SHORT • S
ARN
LUN

PAUL HANNON

# HILLSIDE PUBLICATIONS
2 New School Lane, Cullingworth, Bradford BD13 5DA

First Published 2022  © Paul Hannon 2022

ISBN 978 1 907626 39 5

While the author has walked and researched all these routes for the purposes of this guide, no responsibility can be accepted for any unforeseen circumstances encountered whilst following them

*Sketch maps based on OS 1947 1-inch maps*

Cover illustrations: Devil's Bridge; Arnside
Back cover: Holmepark Fell; Page 1: Silverdale
(Paul Hannon/Yorkshire Photo Library)

Printed in China on behalf of Latitude Press

## HILLSIDE GUIDES... cover much of Northern England

- 50 Yorkshire Walks For All
- Journey of the Wharfe (photobook)

**Short Scenic Walks**
- Teesdale & Weardale
- Ribble Valley & Bowland
- Wharfedale & Ilkley
- Three Peaks & Malham
- Arnside & Lunesdale
- North York Moors
- Harrogate & Nidderdale
- South Pennines
- Wensleydale & Swaledale
- Ambleside & South Lakeland
- Pendle & Lancashire Moors
- Aire Valley
- Haworth

**Walking in Yorkshire**
- North York Moors South & West
- Nidderdale & Ripon
- Wharfedale & Malham
- Aire Valley & Brontë Country
- Yorkshire Wolds
- South Yorkshire
- Three Peaks & Howgill Fells
- North York Moors North & East
- Wensleydale & Swaledale
- Harrogate & Ilkley
- Howardian Hills & Vale of York
- Calderdale & South Pennines
- West Yorkshire Countryside

**Lancashire/Cumbria**  • Pendle & the Ribble  • Eden Valley

**Long Distance**  • Dales Way  • Coast to Coast Walk  • Pendle Way

*Visit us at www.hillsidepublications.co.uk*

# CONTENTS

*River Bela, Dallam Park*
*Stone graves, Heysham*

Introduction...........................4

1  Sizergh Castle.................6
2  River Kent......................8
3  Levens Park...................10
4  Dallam Park & Beetham...12
5  The Fairy Steps..............14
6  Arnside Knott................16
7  Arnside Point................18
8  Around Silverdale..........20
9  Leighton Moss..............22
10 Jenny Brown's Point......24
11 Warton Crag.................26
12 Lancaster Canal............28
13 Hutton Roof Crags........30
14 Clawthorpe Fell............32
15 Holmepark Fell.............34
16 Barbon Low Fell...........36
17 Around Casterton.........38
18 Whittington..................40
19 Leck Beck.....................42
20 Fourstones...................44
21 Wenning's Banks..........46
22 Tatham & Wennington....48
23 Gressingham & the Lune...50
24 Three Rivers.................52
25 Crook o'Lune...............54
26 Littledale......................56
27 Clougha Pike................58
28 Aldcliffe Marsh.............60
29 Sunderland Point..........62
30 Heysham Head.............64

3

# INTRODUCTION

The fascinating countryside where Lancashire and Cumbria meet is hugely diverse, from the western fringes of the Yorkshire Dales and the Bowland moors across Lunesdale to historic Lancaster and Morecambe, then along the coast to Arnside and Silverdale. Half the walks fall within Areas of Outstanding Natural Beauty (Arnside & Silverdale and Forest of Bowland), while four enter the Yorkshire Dales and the Lake District National Parks.

Arnside & Silverdale occupy a superlative setting where the Kent Estuary opens out into Morecambe Bay, an absorbing tangle of limestone outcrops, lush pastures, rich woodland and intriguing seashore beneath iconic Arnside Knott, while Leighton Moss is an internationally important bird reserve. Amid these natural charms are lovely villages such as Beetham, Sandside and Warton, and sumptuous country houses such as Leighton Hall, Dallam Tower, Sizergh Castle and Levens Hall. Across the Lancaster Canal, an almost forgotten waterway whose towpath is a delight to tread, are the spacious limestone heights of Hutton Roof, Clawthorpe and Farleton. They in turn fall towards the River Lune, running from the Yorkshire Dales to Lancaster, with the old market town of Kirkby Lonsdale at its heart. The lovely Lune absorbs the side valleys of the Greta and the Wenning flowing from the Dales and Bowland, with charming villages such as Barbon, Wray and Hornby alongside natural gems such as Leck Beck, Clougha Pike and Littledale.

The majority of walks are on rights of way or established access areas and paths: a handful which cross Open Access land are noted as such, though none of the routes impact on grouse moors. Whilst the route description should be sufficient to guide you around, a map is recommended for greater information and interest: Ordnance Survey Explorer maps OL2, OL7, OL41 and 296 cover the walks.

*Information*
- The Storey, Meeting House Lane **Lancaster** LA1 1TH (01524-582394)
- Old Station Buildings **Morecambe** LA4 4DB (01524-582808)
- 29 Main Street **Kirkby Lonsdale** LA6 2AH (015242-97177)
- 2 Sandylands Road **Kendal** LA9 6EU (01539-736006)
- Town Hall, 8 Station Road **Bentham** LA2 7LF (015242-62549)
- Community Centre Car Park **Ingleton** LA6 3HX (015242-41049)

# ARNSIDE & LUNESDALE
## 30 Short Scenic Walks

Sizergh **1**  **2** Sedgwick
Levens
Bridge **3**
Kent

**16** Barbon

Milnthorpe
**4**   Newbiggin
**15**
**5**                    **17** Kirkby
Sandside         **14**        **18** Lonsdale
Holme   **13**
**6 7**           Hutton           **19** Cowan
Arnside          Roof                  Bridge

Silverdale **8 9**

River Lune

**10** Crag  **12** Tewitfield
Foot
**11**            Melling
Warton              **22**   High
Arkholme **23**        Bentham
**Morecambe**                  Low     **21 20**
**Bay**                   **24** Bentham
Hornby    Wenning

**Morecambe**        Caton
**30**     River Lune  **25**
**28**    Crossgill **26**
**Lancaster**
Quernmore **27**

Middleton
**29**

*The Pepperpot,
Castlebarrow*

5

# 1 SIZERGH CASTLE

**4 miles from Sizergh**

**A one-off excursion into the Lake District National Park**

*Start* Strickland Arms (SD 500873; LA8 8DZ), roadside parking
*Map* OS Explorer OL7, English Lakes South East

The Strickland Arms stands by the entrance to Sizergh Castle on the former course of the A6: under the adjacent A591 bridge is a farm shop. Turn up a side lane right of the pub to cottages, then double back right on the access track in front of them. Up the side bear right to a kissing-gate, behind which planks negotiate a moist corner. A path slants left up the field to a junction: go right, up to meet a wall and follow it outside Chapel Wood to the top corner. You shall return to this point to finish. For now, turn right to a bridle-gate, with Sizergh Castle ahead. Follow the wallside towards it to emerge into its car park. Sizergh is probably the finest house in old Westmorland, its pele tower much added to in Elizabethan times. The house contains an impressive array of treasures, and has been occupied by the Strickland family for over 700 years. In the care of the National Trust, it is open to view, with cafe and shop.

Cross the car park to a gate in the facing wall, with another just ahead into a field. A firm path crosses to the far corner, through the gate joining a track. Follow it right up to a barn, and in the yard take a small gate into a wooded bank. A good path runs at mid-height, rising at the end onto an access track. With Holeslack just ahead, double back briefly right to a gate on the left, and rise left up the field to a stile. Rising slightly further, cross to a farm road and go left on it to a road-end at Helsington church. The lonely church of St John marks the walk's high point, and a view indicator identifies the magnificent array of Lakeland Fells far beyond the Lyth Valley.

Resume by doubling back left on an access road continuing from the surfaced road end, running a wallside course to a bend left. Leaving by a gate in the wall ahead, a broad green way runs along a gentle crest. The wood on the right drops away to give views over the Lyth Valley, then the path drops down a limestone base to a gate. Regaining its broad, grassy surface, drop straight down this vast pasture with a hedge on your right. Shortly after a lesser right branch, the path passes through a gap and away past an isolated boulder. It then swings gently left down this open pasture, with the Kent Estuary leading to Morecambe Bay. Ultimately it slants right down to a corner bridle-gate onto a road by the trees of Brigsteer Park.

From a kissing-gate opposite, a rough track slants left across the field. Towards the end it drops into Cinderbarrow farm: don't follow it in but go left to a wall-stile onto a road. Climb left to an angled crossroads, where a small gate on the left sends a permissive path climbing through parallel limestone bands. Through trees above, it reaches a bridle-gate into a pasture on Sizergh Fell. The path heads away, bearing slightly left to a gate in the wall ahead. The left-hand path heading away curves onto a brow, with a hawthorn-crowned Bronze Age burial mound to your right. The path drops to a bridle-gate in the hedge below, then descends a big pasture, revealing the castle as it curves down to a corner gate by your outward route. Retrace opening steps to finish.

*Sizergh Castle*

# 2 RIVER KENT

3¾ miles from Sedgwick

**Fascinating rambling by a drained canal and a colourful riverbank**

*Start* Force Bridge (SD 507868; LA8 8EA), off A590/A591 roundabout half-mile west of village, laybys
*Map* OS Explorer OL7, English Lakes South East

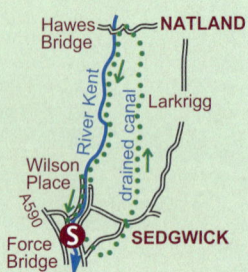

Peering over Force Bridge reveals superb River Kent scenery in the gorge below. From the east side of the bridge, a stile across the road sends a path across a field, with the mansion of Sedgwick House over to the left. Iron kissing-gates see you across a minor road, and the path rises right to a curiously sited stone-arched bridge. This is Sedgwick Hill Bridge, which served to cross the Lancaster Canal whose course you have just reached. Opened in 1819 to link Kendal with Lancaster and further south to Preston, it has been drained since 1955. To your right there is no evidence whatsoever due to infilling, but turning left under the bridge reveals the distinctive, marshy trench of the old waterway.

A firm towpath takes over for a pleasant stroll to Sedgwick, where you find yourself looking down upon this small village from a sturdy aqueduct high above the road. The canal was planned to run further east, but was re-routed through Sedgwick to serve its gunpowder works. Resuming, the former waterway leaves the village on an embankment to emerge into a field, with the canal again infilled. Advance to a kissing-gate, then across a field to pass beneath folly-like Horse Park Bridge. Just beyond, you reach a kissing-gate into the trees of Larkrigg Spring. A deep ditch returns, at the end emerging to run to Larkrigg Hall Bridge. Beyond this the ditch fades again, with Larkrigg Farm to the left. A little further an old milestone set back from the far bank is inscribed '3' and '24', indicating the distances to Kendal and Lancaster.

Crossing the farm drive to a small gate, the way resumes with a boundary still on the left, and at a stile the ditch returns. The grassy embankment leads through successive bridle-gates, with Natland's church tower over to the right beneath the knoll of The Helm. Another infilled section runs the short way to Crowpark Bridge, which carries a road. Passing beneath it, just a few yards further take a kissing-gate on the left onto the road. Turn right down its short, winding course to double-arched Hawes Bridge on the River Kent, with splendid waterplay upstream.

Without crossing, take a stile on the left and head downstream on a fieldside path above the wooded bank. Through a bridle-gate in a wall on a brow the path drops gently, and the trees fade to provide a super short spell above the open bank. At the end is a small gate by a well-placed seat, and the path runs on into the wooded bank for a superb lengthy spell by the lively river, with a series of low waterfalls. Appearing on the opposite bank are the remains of Sedgwick Gunpowder Works. The path eventually emerges onto an enclosed bridleway coming in from the left. Advance downstream along this to a gate ahead, then across one final field, tapering to approach Wilson Place. At the end cross the Kent on an airy suspension footbridge onto a minor road. Go left, still with the Kent's company, ignoring a side road and on to a junction. The start is two minutes to the left. *By the River Kent*

# 3     LEVENS PARK

**3¼ miles from Levens Bridge**

**Genteel walking in delightful parkland above the River Kent**

*Start* Levens Bridge (SD 496852; LA8 8EG), large layby at A6/A590 junction north of Levens Hall
*Map* OS Explorer OL7, English Lakes South East

    From the road junction cross the double-arched bridge over the River Kent, with Levens Hall just across the road to your right. Dating back to the 13th century, the defensive pele tower was substantially added to in Elizabethan times, and is open to the public. Perhaps Levens' most famous feature is its renowned topiary gardens, created around 1700. Here also are a cafe, plant centre and gift shop. A stile on the left puts you into Levens Park, where the Kent performs its swansong. Having been born among high mountains, it bows out in style through delectable parkland. The park is also graced by a shy herd of rare black Fallow deer and by Bagot goats. A path heads away, quickly rising gently on a low bank above the Kent with super vistas of the gracefully sweeping river. Levelling out it veers away from the river, bearing right at a fork to merge into a broad, level track, the Avenue. This runs a dead-straight course between parallel oaks, with the river out of sight in its deep trough. At the very end the river re-appears below, and the path turns right to a stile by a gate out of the park. Rise onto a road and turn left to immediately bridge the A591.

    Across, bear right up wooden steps to a kissing-gate, then rise gently left into the sloping field. The thin path bears left along here below a parallel fence on the course of the Lancaster Canal, opened in 1819 and drained in 1955. The complete absence of the canal at this point is quite bizarre, this infilled section displaying no evidence whatsoever of the former waterway! Beckoning not far ahead is stone-arched Sedgwick Hill Bridge, the first sign of the canal's existence. Peer under it to appreciate the canal's former presence in a deep, marshy cutting on the edge of Sedgwick. Your onward route, however, takes a path dropping left down the field, using iron kissing-gates to cross a minor road. On again, it drops to a stile onto a road junction at Force Bridge.

Cross the bridge above fine river scenery, then turn left on unsigned Force Lane above the lively Kent. On the opposite bank are remains of Basingill Mills, a largely 19th century gunpowder works. With the A591 briefly alongside, the road drops to Force Cottages, just past which it abruptly ends. A surfaced path traverses a walkway high above the river beneath the road bridge, emerging onto the resurrected old road rising to houses at Park Head. After them a stile on the left sends a path across a field to a corner wall-stile. Head away up the long wallside on your left to a stile at the end back into Levens Park. A broad grassy path drops away, quickly swinging right to run a splendid, undulating course at mid height. Reaching a brow with a lovely prospect of the river lazily winding ahead, the path drops to its very bank. At once it then bears right the short way to a stile by a gate back out onto the A6 where you began.

*The River Kent in Levens Park*

# 4     DALLAM PARK & BEETHAM

**4½ miles from Milnthorpe**

**Parkland, woodland and a lovely village: exquisite stuff**

*Start* Village centre
(SD 497814; LA7 7QJ),
Park Road car park
*Map* OS Explorer OL7,
English Lakes South East

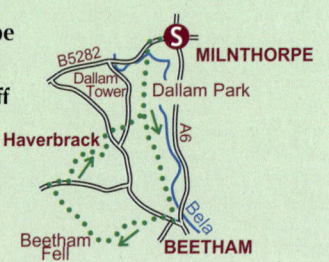

Milnthorpe is a busy village, with shops and pubs in and around its market square. From the crossroads head west on the B5782 footway, and on the village edge cross a bridge over the River Bela into Dallam Park: set back beyond the river is 18th century Dallam Tower. Head directly away up the slope, passing well right of the main brow: the mansion's stately setting is backed by the inner Kent Estuary and the Lakeland Fells. A stone marker cairn beneath steeper slopes on the left indicates a fork to which you will return: for now keep left on a faint path to a dip. To your left is a roofless deer house, with the resident herd of Fallow deer often close by. A second rise leads to another brow, just left of which the park is left by a kissing-gate at a ha-ha. Descend an avenue of trees to a stile/gate onto an access road at Heron Corn Mill, now a paper-making museum with a working waterwheel.

Advance along the access road into Beetham, going right for the village centre. Turn right at the Wheatsheaf Hotel and on between a tearoom in the old Post office and the ancient St Michael's church, a lovely spot. A stile on the left at the village edge sends you up a field centre to one into the woodland of Beetham Fell. The path bears right, quickly rising beneath a ruin. From a corner stile it becomes enclosed to rise past then above it, swinging right to join a cart track. Turn right with an adjacent fence to reach a T-junction of such ways. Go 50 yards left to a crossroads of ways marked by a stone cairn, where turn right on the thinner path to an old wall gateway. It then rises through low outcrops to join a level path to quickly meet a wall on the right.

Rise slightly to pass through a stile just above, then the path rises a very short way onto a broad path on a gentle brow. Ignoring a thinner path ahead, turn right for little over 100 yards to another marker cairn just five yards past a waymarked junction. Here bear left for a grand woodland stroll, gently losing height and passing through a scar before a level section. Joining a cart track bear right past a branch dropping left, and 30 yards further is a cross-paths. Turn right, rising along the edge of a small limestone pavement to quickly reach a stile onto Cockshot Lane. Still amid trees, rise right to a brow, then drop a short way to a stile on the left.

Of two paths heading away, take the broad one ahead. Very slightly rising, it angles right and dead-straight to soon reach a T-junction: go right to drop rapidly to a junction with a broader path. Go right again the short way down to a gate/stile out of the wood, and now enclosed for a short way to join an access road, with Wray Cottage to your right. Go left on this enclosed cart track to the hamlet of Haverbrack, and out on the access road the short way to a through road. A stile in front puts you back into Dallam Park, dropping left near the bottom to a kissing-gate onto a road. From a kissing-gate opposite, bear left to rejoin your outward route at the cairn, and retrace opening steps.

*At Beetham*

# 5 THE FAIRY STEPS

**4¼ miles from Sandside**

**A coastal start leads into rich woodland with a dramatic limestone cleft as centrepiece**

*Start* Ship Inn (SD 477807; LA7 7HW), roadside parking to west
*Map* OS Explorer OL7, English Lakes South East

Sandside is a small village protruding out into Milnthorpe Sands in the Kent Estuary. From the roadside parking head east on the footway, which ends as you make use of a grassy foreshore path before crossing to the Ship Inn. Past its car park a short snicket runs right to a back road, passing a path on the old railway at Sandside Cutting. Turn left for 50 yards on the road, then bear right up a rough road. Quickly leave by a path right, rising through trees to rejoin the firm track. Go right, rapidly levelling to run pleasantly to a T-junction of paths. Turn right, becoming an access road (Yans Lane) past an isolated bungalow on the edge of Storth. Reaching houses, a stile on the left sends an enclosed path to a stile into trees. Rising left past a limestone edge, it swings right to commence a delightful woodland ramble. Ultimately reaching a T-junction of paths, turn right to drop to a stile onto a road through the woods.

Go briefly right to a brow, and take a broad path doubling back left through a stile/gate. This runs an infallible, gently rising course between wall and fence set back. Eventually it levels out on the brow of Beetham Fell to reach a stone marker cairn. At this staggered junction advance a few yards and bear right on a level path through coppiced woodland. With a substantial limestone cliff forming on the left, remain on the main path to meet a descending path. While your continuation is right, first go a few strides left to the foot of the Fairy Steps, a narrow cleft in the limestone cliff, and something of a 'fat man's agony'. Though off-

14

route it would be folly to omit them, so ease your way up to earn a sojourn on open ground above. Resuming, head down the path through Underlaid Wood, quickly encountering a gentler version of the Fairy Steps. Emerging at a gate, a green track runs along fieldsides to a road junction at Hazelslack Tower Farm. Cross over and along the road between farm buildings, dominated by the 14th century pele tower. Just beyond, take a stile on the right and rise left past the foot of the tower to a stile by a gate. Now make for the far end of the larger, hummocky pasture to a stile onto a road.

From a stile opposite follow a track away: as it swings right to become enclosed by walls, bear left to an interesting stile in the wall corner. Now follow the wall on the left beneath a wooded bank, through two long pastures almost entirely enclosed by woodland. Ultimately bear right to a stile into the woods at the far end, from where a short, stony track rises to a gate/stile. Back into daylight, follow the wall on the left again to a stile onto Cockshot Lane. Turn briefly left, then fork right beneath a limestone scar on Throughs Lane to Yans Lane at the top edge of Storth. Go left on the road dropping gently into the centre, down to a junction by the Post office/shop. Cross straight over onto a little green with a war memorial and resume down Green Lane, over the very deep railway cutting down onto the coast road. Cross to the footway and turn right to finish in style.

*Ascending the Fairy Steps*

# 6 ARNSIDE KNOTT

4¾ miles from Arnside

**A steady ascent to an iconic small hill overlooking the Kent Estuary**

*Start* The Pier (SD 456788; LA5 0HA), roadside parking
*Map* OS Explorer OL7, English Lakes South East

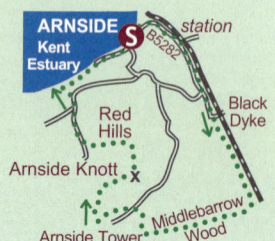

Arnside is a charming little resort, with pubs, shops and cafes strung along the seafront. Here the Kent Estuary gives way to the waters of Morecambe Bay, the 50-arched Kent Viaduct proving an arbitrary border. From the tiny pier, head right to a bend by the car park near the viaduct, and go right on the footway past the rail station to a junction. Keep straight on through a linear garden to resume on suburban Black Dyke Road. As it swings left at the end to a level-crossing at Black Dyke, a cart track on the right swings left to farm buildings. Between them a thin path runs to a bridle-gate into the edge of Hagg Wood, parallel with the railway.

Quickly leaving the wood, a farm road is crossed and an open section ensues alongside a lengthy pasture, still by the railway. Ahead is Middlebarrow Wood, with Arnside Tower dramatically revealed over to the right. Over a footbridge on a drain, resume to one at the end into the wood. Advance for a minute then double sharply back right on a level path running near the wood edge. A lengthy stroll leads all the way to emerge via a gate/stile facing Arnside Tower Farm, backed by the steep Shilla Slopes on the flank of Arnside Knott. Just up to your left, 14th century Arnside Tower was a pele tower for defence against marauding Scots. Pass left of the farm buildings to join a track, across which a bridle-gate sends an enclosed path along to join the drive. Rise left the short way onto a road, and cross to a bridle-gate into Arnside Knott Wood.

The broad track of Saul's Drive slants gently left through the trees, through a gate and curving right up onto a minor brow. Here turn right, a gate/kissing-gate sending a firm path rising away. Over a level cross-path it winds up through increasingly open terrain, a steeper spell leading to a bench on a knoll, with a broad track just behind. Turn right on this with estuary views, rising very slightly to pass the remains of a knotted larch tree, a Victorian landmark: just beyond is another viewpoint seat. While you could advance straight on here, a lesser path branches right for the minute's rise to a broader track, rising briefly right to the OS column at 521ft/159m crowning Arnside Knott, entirely screened by scrub.

The broad track drops back down to meet the main, level one, running just 20 yards further to a rustic gate accessing the walk's highlight. This stunning moment reveals an exquisite, far-reaching panorama across the vast open slopes of Red Hills. The Kent Viaduct and the spacious estuary are foreground to an array of Lakeland Fells. Leave by the broad green path slanting gently right, and tread slowly to savour this classic scene. In line with a kissing-gate in a wall that comes in on the right, take a level, grassy branch left. This runs a delectable course across the lower slopes to a kissing-gate onto a road. Turn down this to meet a suburban road, and go briefly right to the dip. Here drop left between houses to a surfaced path down onto the foreshore, another fine moment. Turn right on the beach and follow the part stony shore back into Arnside, becoming firmer as you approach the Coastguard station with refreshments behind.

*The Kent Estuary from Arnside Knott*

# 7 ARNSIDE POINT

**3½ miles from Arnside**

**A beautiful coastal walk beneath Arnside Knott's colourful flanks**

*Start* Arnside Knott (SD 450774; LA5 0BP), National Trust car park at end of a cul-de-sac road reached by Silverdale Road and Red Hills Road south-west of village
*Map* OS Explorer OL7, English Lakes South East

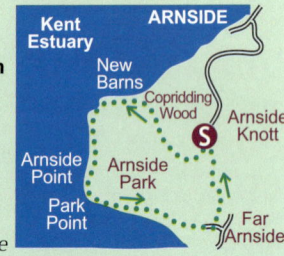

At the end of the car park, a wooden gate in a wall sends a broad path dropping gently away through scattered trees to another wall-gate. The path then drops a little further, soon down to a cross-paths in front of dense woodland. Turn sharp right here, rapidly emerging into open country, the surroundings of scattered trees, scrub and bracken further enhanced by views over the Kent Estuary. The path drops into trees and through a gate in a wall, maintaining a sustained drop through Copridding Wood. Towards the bottom it slants right towards a gate out of the trees: don't use it, but take a fenced path to its right between fields to a kissing-gate onto a narrow road. Turn briefly left to emerge onto the edge of New Barns Bay, a super moment. The concrete road runs left to cottages at New Barns, where bear right onto the grassy foreshore.

This area is notorious for exceptionally fast-rising tides, quicksands and hidden channels: under no circumstances wander aimlessly out onto sandbanks without awareness of tide times. A super walk leads around to Blackstone Point, either on a lovely greensward or broad sands beneath shoreline cliffs fronting Frith Wood (if high tides preclude this, a woodland path runs from New Barns to White Creek to then use a clifftop path). Soon reaching the arc of White Creek's modest inlet, at low water it's simply a matter of striding out on the firm sands to Arnside Point just across it, though one has the option of a grassy path beneath the scrub and cliffs, or even up onto the path above. Shortly after Arnside Point the grassy sward ends beneath cliffs, and assuming you're still safely on the shore, you'll quickly reach an unmissable tilted rocky spit, with its inviting natural slant up onto the clifftop path.

Turn right for a splendid march along the crest on the edge of the woodland of Arnside Park, to pass an inviting grassy knoll above the distinct corner of Park Point. Whilst the path is good, small children shouldn't be running around too giddily. Cliffs and path now swing back left to reveal the Silverdale shoreline. This mercurial section runs into trees to finally rise left to meet another path at a gate in a wall. Pass through on a short, level stroll to an exclusive caravan park. Follow the upper road heading away through the site to emerge at the houses at Far Arnside. Leaving the site advance just a short way along the lane, then a stile/gate on the left send an enclosed path rising to the farm at Hollins. A stile admits onto its drive, but turn immediately left past the barns, through a gate and up an enclosed little way to a gate into the extensive open pasture of Heathwaite. Turn right on the broad path alongside a wall, ascending in increasing style to a crossroads with the bridleway of Saul's Drive at the top. Go left on this broad track, soon dropping right away from the wall to run to a gate in another wall. Through it head away on a gentle rise the short way to the next one, with the car park just behind.

*At Arnside Point*

19

# 8 AROUND SILVERDALE

**3¾ miles from Silverdale**

**Coastal and woodland paths link the scattered Silverdale scene**

*Start* Eaves Wood (SD 471759; LA5 0UQ), National Trust car park between village and station
*Map* OS Explorer OL7, English Lakes South East

Rejoin the road and head away on a narrow side road, The Row. Part way along the houses, a private-looking gate on the left sends a path between gardens into woodland. Heading away, keep right to drop to a fence-stile before turning right to enter a trough. A cart track merges to lead out onto a road: turn briefly left to a stile on the right, sending a path outside a house into trees. Ignoring a branch dropping right, you soon descend steps to a small gate into Lambert's Meadow. Cross to a footbridge, then left with the streamlet to a kissing-gate into trees at the substantial Burton Well. A broad path heads away between cliffs and wall, rising gently then swinging right between walls to Burtonwell Cottage. Its short drive joins Bottoms Lane at Silverdale Green: go left, soon turning right on The Green to join Stankelt Road.

Turn right for a suburban half-mile to a junction, with the heart of Silverdale village on your right. Here are the Royal pub, a Post office, shops, cafe and WC. Take the road dropping left, keeping right at a junction and dropping past the Silverdale Hotel. Swing right at the bottom to end on Silverdale's beach, a lovely moment. Head right along the foreshore, quickly becoming a short beach walk beneath cliffs to swing in to a prominent inlet at The Cove: note the cliff-cave ahead. Turn up into this hollow to the base of Cove Lane, rising onto Cove Road. Turning right, a verge path soon starts on the left to run to a stile at the start of a snicket. This leads between houses onto Wallings Lane: advance briefly along, then keep straight on the access road ahead. This ends at a house, where a small gate in front accesses another snicket. Quickly absorbing a drive this runs to the top of Elmslack Lane, where turn left into a corner of Eaves Wood.

Turn right on the path along the base of the wood. Rapidly entering a walled section, instead take a path climbing left to a junction, where rise gently left to reach a distinctive gnarled beech tree. While the path swings right, an initially less obvious one rises left of the tree through scattered limestone, quickly becoming clear to run to a fork just short of a junction with a broader path. Rise left the few strides to a path crossroads and guidepost, to which you will return after the two-minute detour left up a path to the Pepperpot on the limestone crest of Castlebarrow. The monument of 1887 commemorates Queen Victoria's Golden Jubilee, and enjoys big views over Silverdale's wooded and coastal delights. Returning to the broader path at the junction below, turn right along it on the edge of a large clearing to a gateway in a wall. Through it fork right, slanting onto a broad, level path, and go left for a grand stride. Swinging right at a junction, it doubles back right down to fork left above a waymarked path junction. At the guidepost slant left gently downhill on the main path, onto a level, equally broad one. Go left for a lengthier stroll nearing the wood bottom, reaching a junction where turn right to drop back to the car park.

*On Silverdale shore, looking to Arnside Knott*

21

# 9 LEIGHTON MOSS

**4¼ miles from Silverdale**

**Absorbing features above an iconic RSPB nature reserve**

**Start** Railway station (SD 476751; LA5 0SP), limited roadside parking (nearby RSPB car park is for reserve visitors/members only)
**Map** OS Explorer OL7, English Lakes South East

From the station walk south to the junction, then left on Storrs Lane over the railway and past the visitor centre at Myers Farm with shop and cafe. Leighton Moss is a famous Royal Society for the Protection of Birds reserve known for its elusive bitterns, while avocets and marsh harriers might also be seen. Originally a tidal inlet, by the mid 19th century the moss had silted up such that it was only flooded by high spring tides. Drainage ceased in the 1910s, and the re-flooded moss again became a wildlife haven of shallow meres and reedbeds: it came into the RSPB's care in the 1960s. Turn off right at the first chance alongside a house, and a broad causeway sets off across the moss, passing a public hide. At the end the track enters a field to climb to Grisedale Farm, above which its access road rises to buildings at Home Farm. Just a little further, a cattle-grid is crossed and Leighton Hall appears on the right. This imposing 18th century mansion is open to visitors, along with grounds and gardens, tearoom and birds of prey.

Ignoring the driveway through parkland in front, bear left to a small gate to climb steeply and sometimes faintly, slanting steadily right to the top. Seats here offer an ideal break to appraise the hall's enviable setting, with a backdrop of Morecambe Bay and the Lakeland Fells beyond Arnside Knott. Resuming, ignore the main path right along the crest of the hill, and take a kissing-gate into the field behind. Cross straight over Summerhouse Hill to the mound of an ancient burial cairn. Behind it the path winds steeply down a small bank, through an old wall towards a stile onto a lane climbing out of Yealand Conyers. Don't use it but go left on a path above a fence, quickly running to an old iron gate into trees. It runs more broadly on, dropping to the end where a gate puts you onto a grassy cart track at a field edge. Follow its nice course the length of this island pasture surrounded by woodland.

Through a gate towards the tapering end, advance a short way further on this narrow strip between trees. Faced with another gate, instead take a stile on the left fronting a small limestone scar. Up its natural staircase, a path drops through Deepdale Wood to a small gap in a wall, then slants left through scrub along a linear clearing. Soon reaching a rocky bluff, the path drops sharply right into the deep bowl of Deep Dale, with reed-choked Deepdale Pond surrounded by springtime bluebells. The path circles around its left side and rises slightly to meet a broader path. Turn left to a slight brow amid lichen-covered limestone. Dropping gently to a T-junction with a broader track, go left to quickly reach another junction where the track goes left: your path is straight ahead, dropping to a gate into a field. Crossing to another opposite, your objective is a gate back onto the access road at Home Farm, visible down the field. The unseen right of way slants down the field to the gate, though across the field a wallside track drops right down to it too. Turn right to retrace steps via Grizedale Farm and the causeway.

*Leighton Moss*

23

# 10    JENNY BROWN'S POINT

**4$^1$4 miles from Crag Foot**

**Fascinating Silverdale coast and country**

**Start** Morecambe Bay nature reserve (SD 475737; LA5 9SA), RSPB car park under railway west of hamlet
**Map** OS Explorer OL7, English Lakes South East

From the car park return through the gateway and straight ahead on a bridge over a drain. Turn left on a grassy embankment at Quaker's Stang, a permissive path that beyond an early gate swings right to a kissing-gate at the base of Heald Brow. At this cross-paths turn left between a sandy channel and the scrubby bank, opening out for a lovely greensward stroll to a landmark chimney from an old copper-smelting mill. Just past it are isolated Brown's Houses, whose narrow access road heads away above the rocky shore. Soon reaching a corner above Jenny Brown's Point, the road turns inland. After a stile onto the point (viewing a stone embankment extending into the bay) is a kissing-gate into the National Trust's promontory of Jack Scout, a colourful scrub and limestone pasture. Turn right on the main path to a small gate in a fence, through which fork left, soon reaching a clearing revealing a massive sweep of the bay. Joining a fence above modest cliffs, this runs a super course overlooking the bay. At a substantial inlet at the end, veer right through bracken to reach an impressive limekiln, behind which is a kissing-gate back onto the lane.

Go left past Gibraltar Farm to a junction with a through road at Wolf House Gallery (both with refreshments). Keep left on Lindeth Road towards Silverdale, and at the first opportunity turn right on narrow Woodwell Lane into trees. As it rises to a slight brow with a house set back to the right, turn left on a path to a wall-stile to run an enclosed course through trees to Woodwell

Cottage. Just yards along its drive resume on an enclosed path through trees, becoming a tall-walled snicket, crossing a driveway, and on again to emerge between houses onto an access road rising onto Stanklet Road in Silverdale. The village centre is just one minute to the left, where two hotels, the Silverdale and the Royal, offer refreshment, along with a cafe, Post office, shops and WC.

Your route is right for a few minutes through suburbia, until reaching The Chase on the right. Immediately after it an enclosed path runs to a stile, then right along a field edge to one into trees. Going left along its edge, you reach a kissing-gate into a long pasture: rapidly forking, bear right to one back into trees. A good path heads away to an outer wall corner, then continues on the wood edge again with the wall on your left and Woodwell Cliff down to your right. At the end is a stile onto Hollins Lane. Just a few yards right, a gate opposite sends a path the few strides to a gate ahead, accessing an inviting enclosed path. At the end take a bridle-gate on the left, and the way runs a few strides further to one into a field. Head away with the wall on your right, on a further fieldside to a stile onto colourful Heald Brow. A clear path heads away, bearing gently right and dropping slightly to a small gate in a wall. A sustained descent of the scrubby bank emerges at the path crossroads by the early kissing-gate. Retrace steps on the embankment to finish.

*Smelt mill chimney, Brown's Houses*

# 11     WARTON CRAG

**4¾ miles from Warton**

**Delightful limestone country**

*Start* Village centre (SD 498723; LA5 9PJ), car park on Crag Road 50 yards off main street
*Map* OS Explorer OL7, English Lakes South East

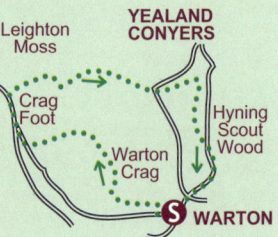

Warton's centre features the George Washington pub, Old School Brew House, St Oswald's church, 700-year old Rectory and Post office/shop. A path from the car park rises beneath a quarried wall to a stile onto a broader path. Turn right up through a kissing-gate into a corner of Warton Crag nature reserve, where the path splits. Take the left branch slanting up into open surrounds, and at the start of a low limestone terrace take the upper path along its crest. Views range from Ingleborough to the Bowland moors, with Morecambe Bay outspread. Maintain this splendid, steady rise to a kissing-gate above a massive old quarry. A path heads away outside its fence: within thirty yards branch right to rise steadily through further limestone to the base of a larger cliff. A stile sees the path make an easy passage between the rocks onto gentler ground. Ignoring a fork right, it runs on to rise the short way to outcrops forming a super viewpoint over the bay. Just to the right is a fork alongside the Beacon, and a few yards right amid dense scrub, an OS column marks Warton Crag's summit at 534ft/163m.

From the beacon fork left on a good path through scrub, and ignoring an early lesser right fork, it gently declines into trees and along to a gate in a wall. A grass track heads away through more open country, dropping left to run to a gate onto Occupation Road, an enclosed bridleway. Turn left for a sustained descent onto Crag Road, then right down to a junction at Crag Foot. Here stands a chimney from a pump-house built to aid drainage of Leighton Moss. Without joining the through road take the access road right, and just short of Moss House Farm, turn right up an enclosed stony track. Quickly back into trees it rises away, then forks as the main way curves right to a paintball centre. Take the more inviting left option to a gate/stile out of the trees. Joining another track, cross the pasture to a gate/stile in the top corner, looking down on Leighton Moss. It then rises between fences, and just short of a gate, leave it for a grassy option through a gate to its left. This faint way runs along a lengthy pasture outside a wood to a gate at the far end. Now pathless, head across the centre of this big sloping pasture, veering gently right towards the end as you approach a wood. In scattered trees a clear path forms, and rises the short way to a wall-stile. Above it turn left on a field-edge cart track, soon becoming enclosed to emerge onto a road.

From a gate/stile opposite, head away with a hedge to a corner gate. A faint grassy way heads away, passing an immense limekiln then on through two wooded bands of limestone before dropping to another at a corner of the Woodland Trust's Hyning Scout Wood. Just a little further is a stile into it, and within yards you have three options. Take the central path heading away along a gentle crest, on a super course to ultimately gently drop to meet a broader path at the wood edge. Turn left, quickly arriving at a gate. Through this a walled way gently descends the wood edge, passing another mighty limekiln just short of the road. Turn right, all the way back along Main Street into the centre.

*On Warton Crag*

# 12 LANCASTER CANAL

4¼ miles from Tewitfield

**A delectable canal towpath leads to further interesting features**

*Start* *Longlands Hotel (SD 519736; LA6 1JH), roadside parking by marina off A6070 alongside M6 bridge*
*Map* *OS Explorer OL7, English Lakes South East*

From the hotel follow the short access road to the Lancaster Canal at Tewitfield Basin. Construction of the M6 in 1968 wreaked havoc on the hapless waterway, leaving this the northern limit of navigation. Just under the road bridge to your right is the start of the Northern Reaches, where eight defunct locks remain in place. The canal from Preston opened in 1797, though it was a further 22 years before this now severely fractured section reached Kendal. A long-term scheme aims to fully restore the waterway. Turn left around the canal head and head south on the towpath, opposite the marina. So begins a delightful stroll of some 1½ miles amid open countryside, passing beneath several neat bridges. Passing a milestone comes a tiny arm that served a limestone quarry, then on to moorings by a caravan park. Passing beneath a rail bridge you cross the single-span Keer Aqueduct, carrying the waterway 35ft/11m over the modest River Keer. Just beyond it, leave the towpath on steps up to Bridge 131 at Capernwray.

Turn left over the bridge, and sharp left on an access road, re-crossing the aqueduct to the rail bridge at the caravan park entrance. Without passing under, turn right on a short grassy way into a field. Now simply follow a little path beneath the unseen railway and above the Keer valley. Ahead, the Dales fells of Great Coum and Gragareth are quickly joined by Ingleborough's flat top. Just short of the end drop right to a stile, with a streamlet bridge to a stile into another field. Head away with the hedge on your right to a corner gate, with the Keer to your right. Now bear left on a faint way across this large pasture, curving round the base of the gentle slope on your left to a far corner gate/stile. An enclosed way heads away to pass beneath a tall railway arch, then rises to farm buildings at Green Bank. At the top, enter the yard in front then go right the short way out onto a road. Turn left for half a mile into scattered Borwick, with Borwick Hall appearing on your left. This magnificent building incorporates a 14th century pele tower and Elizabethan great hall: just along the side road, a gatehouse through which you might glimpse the hall front bears a 1650 datestone. It is currently an outdoor education centre.

Advance past the little green to a second junction, with a second green on your right. At its end bear left on a short access road between houses. Quickly ending, go right on a grassy way behind a barn, on through a stile and above further farm buildings. A scrubby corner is crossed to a stile, with another just above. Bear right up the steep pasture, with views beyond Priest Hutton to Farleton and Holmepark Fells. Cross to a stile in a tiny length of wall ahead, and follow the hedge away. Quickly using a stile in it, a brief narrow section runs on into a field. Resume with the hedge to a stile onto the bridleway of Kirkgate Lane. Turn left to a gentle brow, then descend pleasantly to emerge alongside Tewitfield Methodist Church. Cross the adjacent canal bridge to finish on the towpath as you began.

*The Lancaster Canal at Borwick*

29

# 13 HUTTON ROOF CRAGS

**3½ miles from Hutton Roof**

**An absorbing tract of limestone upland with magnificent views**

*Start* Village centre (SD 570783; LA6 2PG), roadside parking, village hall car park (when not in use)
*Map* OS Explorer OL7, English Lakes South East

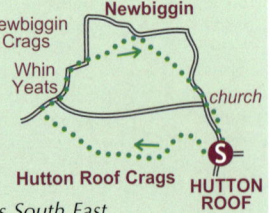

Hutton Roof is a small settlement beneath the limestone heights of Hutton Roof Crags. From the central junction, go a few steps along the street and turn up the enclosed drive of Crag Lane. Ending at a house, take the gate in front into the open country of Hutton Roof Crags. This colourful area is designated a Site of Special Scientific Interest, dominated by limestone crags, pavements, scars and boulders in amongst rich vegetation. A path briefly rises away then swings left, then rapidly right to immediately fork. Looking back, the tip of Ingleborough joins other fells on view. Take the right branch, rising gently through scrub beneath a craggy scarp and on to quickly emerge to cross a more open section through bracken. As paths come in from the right, the path begins to climb by a wall, and a little higher it becomes grassy for a lovely climb as it diverges slightly from the wall. Look back to a fine prospect of the Howgill Fells, Middleton Fell and Great Coum.

On easing, but before the brow, the path forks. Take the left branch rising more steeply through a minor nick to level out and reach a T-junction. Go right, swinging briefly uphill to an early fork. Take the firmer right one slanting more gently up: the left option accesses The Rakes, a line of tilted crags. Looking back to Ingleborough joining the other Dales fells, this slant quickly eases to gain the walk's highest point. This brow enjoys extensive views, with a massive Lakeland skyline beyond neighbouring Farleton Fell, and the Bowland moors to the south beyond your own immediate landscape of limestone and scrub.

The path resumes to soon commence a very steady descent, with higher ground on your left and modest limestone and scrub on the right. Over a lesser cross-path you soon enter increasingly denser scrub for a lengthy level section. Ultimately emerging into the open, it slants gently right down into increasing bracken and then further scrub. At a fork, ignore the level left branch and continue down into a little more scrub, merging with a wall for the final few strides to a kissing-gate onto the crest of a road.

Turn right to drop to a fork at Whin Yeats, and bear left to descend its narrow course to a junction at the bottom. Go straight ahead on a hedgerowed cart track, dropping a little further then rising to a gate by a ramshackle barn. The wallside track continues through two fields to a gate at the end, and a short, walled way leads to a gate onto a bend of Newbiggin Lane. Without joining the road take a narrow, hedgerowed path rising away. This remains your course for a lengthy spell, eventually levelling out with big views left from the Howgill Fells to Ingleborough. Finally emerging onto a road, turn right the short way to a junction by St John's church. The village hall is just a minute further, but if returning to the centre, take a stile on the left opposite the church and cross to another, with yet another just behind. Turn right on the grassy hedgerowed way to emerge back onto the road, with the village centre two minutes further.

*Farleton Fell from Hutton Roof Crags*

# 14 CLAWTHORPE FELL

4$^3$4 miles from Holme

**Rich variety between two neighbouring villages, from limestone nature reserve to canal towpath**

*Start* Village centre (SD 524788; LA6 1PS), roadside parking/car park
*Map* OS Explorer OL7, English Lakes South East

Leave by the Burton Road between the Smithy Inn/shop and Holy Trinity church, its footway leading to a bridge on the Lancaster Canal. Don't cross but turn down steps to join the towpath, and turn right for a delightful 1$^1$4 miles. Early features are the remains of Holme coke ovens on the opposite bank, while just beyond, cottages and bridge at Sheernest form an attractive scene. Down to the right a little further is a large pond at Holme Mills. A little after Burton village is glimpsed across the M6, an isolated house appears on the opposite bank: just before it, take a stepped path doubling back down onto Station Lane. Turn under the aqueduct, and up over the motorway to the village edge. At an old sign still pointing to the long-closed station, bear right for the centre.

Burton-in-Kendal is a splendid village on the old Lancaster to Kendal coaching route. The Kings Arms survives from those days, while handsome 18th century houses, some with balconies, stand back from the Market Square with its 18th century cross to your right. The church of St James is at the village's northern limit. Go left on the main street past the Post office/shop, village hall and school to a crossroads, and go right up Vicarage Lane. Leave by a track on the left between houses just after Vicarage Close. This is Slape Lane, which swings right to run a firm, level hedgerowed course for a considerable time, soon narrowing to the point where vegetation can become a little claustrophobic in late summer.

Gaining a little height, woodland comes in on the left, and you run as far as a junction with a firm track from the left just as your track starts to climb again through trees. Through a gate your new track runs on to emerge from woodland, passing a fine limekiln to approach Oakwood Farm at Clawthorpe. Advance straight through the yard, crossing at the end to a small gate onto a minor road.

Turn right, up to the end of the few houses opposite. A woodland track goes left alongside Holme Park Quarry nature reserve. Don't enter the reserve on the right, but follow the level, enclosed track through trees. At the end it emerges into a clearing on Clawthorpe Fell National Nature Reserve, revealing a spectacular, tilted limestone pavement. Rare flowers survive in gaps in the rock, where shrubs and small trees also gain a foothold. The faint path bears gently left to contour across the slabs to a wall at the far side. Bear left as a clear path runs into undergrowth to a wall-stile, then heads away outside the working quarry. Soon dropping left, it quickly leaves the wood at a stile/gate. Advance along a grassy fieldside track to a gate/stile back onto the A6070. Go left for 200 yards and turn right on the Holme road (B6384), bridging the M6. As it swings right to the village edge, turn left down Sheernest Lane to the canal bridge, and rejoin the towpath for five minutes back to the opening bridge.

*The Lancaster Canal at Sheernest*

33

# 15 HOLMEPARK FELL

**3½ miles from Newbiggin**

**Easy walking amid stunning limestone scenery with panoramic views**

***Start*** *Whin Yeats (SD 551788; LA6 2PJ), roadside parking on west side of minor Newbiggin-Clawthorpe road summit at Point 192m south of Whin Yeats Farm: easiest approach from Clawthorpe side*
***Map*** *OS Explorer OL7, English Lakes South East*
***Access*** *Open Access land*

From the road summit drop east a few yards to a gate on the left into the open pasture of Newbiggin Crags. Take the left-hand grassy way heading away, but quickly leave its direct march for the hill by forking left on a level course. At an early fork keep right, running on to a grassy cart track rising from the road. Cross straight over, and faintly on to a bridle-gate in a wall. A clear path drops across a pasture to a gate ahead, sending a good track off through open country. This descends grandly and runs on to a gate onto the National Trust's Holmepark Fell. At once the track forks: remain on the main one straight ahead, quickly joining a grassy cart track outside tree-masked Holme Park Quarry. After a level spell it drops gently and stonily, with an old limekiln down to the right. Just short of a corner gate, double back right on a more inviting track to begin a long, steady rise beneath Holmepark Fell's tilted scars.

The way narrows but is always evident on a sustained rise through splendid surrounds for ¾-mile to the very felltop. With a constant escarpment to your right, a lower one soon forms to your left, making a dramatic foreground to views across to Morecambe Bay and the Lakeland Fells, while a narrower section adds further interest. The high point is gained as a wall appears just ahead, with Farleton Fell's sizeable cairn set back across it. Rounded boulders just yards up to your right mark the walk's summit at 869ft/265m, adding Ingleborough and the rolling western Yorkshire Dales fells to the view. Tilted pavements dropping away east beneath your feet form a stunningly rugged landscape. Leave by advancing to the wall ahead, following it briefly right to a stile where you trade Holmepark Fell for Farleton Fell. Meeting a path on its other side, your onward route is right, but to include Farleton Fell's slightly lower top on Farleton Knott go left to a tiny brow, the path crossing a grassy dip and briefly up the other side to the distinctive cairn.

Back at the stile, resume down the path with a superior tilted pavement on your left. At its foot the path forks: take the left branch leaving the wall and rising a few feet to run a classic, level course with outcrops to your right and big views left. Just 50 yards short of a wall, it swings right uphill: leave it here by a thinner but clear path dropping left through outcrops. It zigzags down the short way onto a level, grassy track on a shelf. Turn right on this through a gate in the wall, with its massive natural gatepost. Remain on this delectable grassy way for a long, level stroll, with gorse bushes set back in profusion. Eventually reaching a fork where the main way drops left, keep straight on your level path to resume as before. Reaching an outer wall corner, the path continues above the wall to lead back to the gate where you began. *On Holmepark Fell*

35

# 16                           BARBON LOW FELL

4¼ miles from Barbon

**Superb Dales scenery in an unfrequented corner of the National Park**

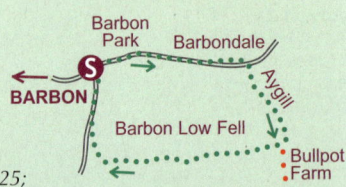

**Start** *Barbondale (SD 637825; LA6 2LG), layby at cattle grid ¾-mile east of village on Dent road*
**Map** *OS Explorer OL2, Yorkshire Dales South/West*
**Access** *Open Access land, no dogs*

    Unassuming Barbon nestles in a fine Lune Valley setting beneath the Dales' westernmost fells: here are the Barbon Inn, tearoom/shop and St Bartholomew's church. Above the parking area is a junction at the foot of Barbon Low Fell: go east on the Dentdale road's verges for a long mile into Barbondale. Barbon Manor is seen in trees across this lower section of the valley, and a circular sheepfold is passed. When the nearby wall drops away take an inviting grass track parallel with it, and at an early fork take the right branch back up to the road. Cross over to a bridleway rising up the lower contours of Barbon Low Fell. This offers fine views north to Middleton Fell, with the side valley of Aygill to your left. The improving track eases on leaving bracken and runs to a gate where it becomes enclosed: this is your turning point. An optional half-hour detour through the gate leads to Bullpot Farm, a caving club base. A kissing-gate to its left sends a wallside path the two minutes along to Bull Pot of the Witches, a forbidding hole dropping 200ft/60m: a waterfall sometimes pours over the lip.
    Back at the gate turn up grassy slopes on the near side of the wall, intermittent trods offering options to ease progress: you might opt to stray further from the wall on a trod slanting towards a telegraph pole, then rising more directly above it to close in on the wall again with a few rocks over to your right. Here a minor knoll is gained to earn a first view of the felltop across a modest saddle. A tiny descent sends you off again, curving away from the

36

wall then gently back to it for the tiny rise to rejoin it. The fell's high point at 1410ft/430m is marked by a small cairn just a few strides up from the wall. This splendid viewpoint features Bowland, Morecambe Bay, the Lakeland Fells across the Lune Valley, Middleton Fell, Barbondale, Baugh Fell, Crag Hill and Gragareth.

Resume by the wall, now pathless as you dip to skirt a marsh and up to a minor knoll. This overlooks an appreciable drop with extensive Nanslope Moss below right. Descend near the wall, then follow trods slightly away from it to enjoy drier ground along the flank of a very gentle spur. At the end is a wall corner at a wall junction, with heathery Casterton Fell on the other side. At this corner go right with the wall, a distinct trod shadowing it round two bends. Just ahead a fence replaces the wall, and the stream transforms into the broadening ravine of Grove Gill, with big Lune Valley views opening out. This now super little path traces it down steeper slopes, leaving the ravine and dropping further right to enter bracken above a large old sheepfold.

From its right side the thinner path slants below it towards a walled plantation, but at a fork before it drop right to cross a stream in front of a bracken-choked fold. Behind it a track runs left, soon bearing right as a super green way slanting down through bracken. Ignoring two distinct branches left, maintain this slant to join an unfenced road at a parking area on the base of the fell. Turn right to finish.

*Barbon Low Fell*

# 17 AROUND CASTERTON

**3¾ miles from Kirkby Lonsdale**

**Easy rambling to an attractive village**

*Start* Devil's Bridge (SD 615782; LA6 2SE), roadside parking off A65
*Map* OS Explorer OL2, Yorkshire Dales South/West

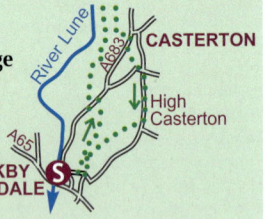

Devil's Bridge is Kirkby Lonsdale's best-known landmark, its three 15th century arches spanning a lively reach of the Lune: it was by-passed in 1932. A refreshment van and WC do brisk trade. From the east side cross the Sedbergh road and go along a section of old road. As it swings right to the A65, turn left up the narrowest of lanes. As it winds up take a kissing-gate left into a caravan site, and head away up to the site shop. Pass to its right, and keep left a few yards further along a site road before branching right the few yards to the hedgerowed bridleway of Laitha Lane. Turn left on this splendid way, rising very gently and swinging right at the end to a junction. Go left past Casterton golf course onto the A683 alongside the clubhouse with cafe: just to the right is a former tollhouse.

Cross to a verge and go left before escaping right at a kissing-gate. Cross to a fence and go right with it towards Casterton Hall, and a kissing-gate puts you onto the drive. Go briefly right to a junction, then double back left on another driveway above wooded grounds. This drops to Mill Hill House: don't enter but take a little path right to a kissing-gate into a field. Follow the wood edge away, at a bend taking a kissing-gate into the trees. A cart track goes right above a wooded gill, and as it merges into a firmer drive, turn off left to bridge the stream. A path heads away through trees to a stile/gate at the other side, then bear right cross open pasture to one back into trees. A path heads away to a kissing-gate into a field corner. Turn right outside the wood, and right on to the end to approach a large house, The Grange.

From a gate at the wood end, advance a short way on a grass track, then turn right through a gate before the grounds. Through another gate, gently descend with a wall on your left to cross a pond outflow to a stile/gate. A path rises to a house, and a hedge leads on between sports fields to a gate into Casterton School grounds. Cross over, down between houses into a yard and down steps to a lower yard. Cross the drive behind to a snicket up between gardens onto the A683 in Casterton. Dominated by its girls' school dating from 1833, Holy Trinity church dates from the same time. Go right past a small green and the Pheasant Inn, and after Town End garage/shop a stile sends an enclosed path left past gardens to a kissing-gate into a field. Bear left to another and on to one just beyond, then bear left to a final one onto Colliers Lane. Go left to a crossroads, then right past prestigious dwellings at High Casterton.

At a cluster of houses just short of a junction, turn right on a dead-end road. Past several houses it becomes a grassy track, dropping between hedgerows to a bend. From a stile on the left a trod rises to the brow of the field, a fine viewpoint for Hutton Roof Crags, the Howgill Fells, Middleton Fell and Casterton Fell. Slant left down to a corner stile, descend to a kissing-gate into a log cabin enclosure, and on to another before a stile back onto Laitha Lane. Go left and remain on the bridleway to a junction at the site entrance. Don't join the road ahead, but turn right down the very narrow lane on which you began.

*The Pheasant, Casterton*

# 18 WHITTINGTON

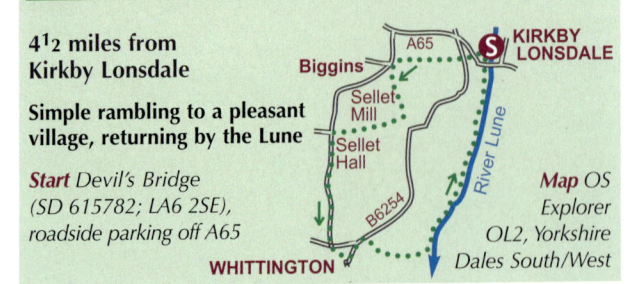

**4½ miles from Kirkby Lonsdale**

**Simple rambling to a pleasant village, returning by the Lune**

**Start** *Devil's Bridge (SD 615782; LA6 2SE), roadside parking off A65*

**Map** *OS Explorer OL2, Yorkshire Dales South/West*

Kirkby Lonsdale is a splendid little market town high above the Lune, with shops, pubs and cafes radiating from a market square. Devil's Bridge is its best-known landmark, its three 15th century arches spanning a lively reach of the river. By-passed in 1932, a refreshment van and WC do brisk trade. From the town end of the bridge take steps downstream into an amenity area, and bear right to a kissing-gate onto the main road. From one opposite rise up the field to one above, sending a snicket between houses onto the B6254. Opposite is the fifth kissing-gate in five minutes, from where a path steeply ascends a field. Easing before reaching the brow, advance with a slim wood to your left. Views to the right look over town up to the Howgill Fells and Middleton Fell, and back around to Casterton Fell and Gragareth.

Now level, pass through successive gates before passing the farm at Wood End over the wall. Just short of the corner, take a gate in the wall and bear right across a limestone enclosure to a kissing-gate onto the drive. Cross straight over, passing a cottage to a narrow, enclosed bridleway dropping gently away. A streamlet comes in to share its course, then as it runs into an old millpond, the path bears right to run to a gate into the environs of Sellet Mill to the left. From a stile on the right, follow the hedgeside as far as a gate in it past a modern house. Through it cross the field to one opposite, with Ingleborough rising impressively to the left. Across a streamlet bear right to join a hedge: as it swings left before reaching trees, take a stile in it and head away with the fence outside the grounds of Sellet Hall on your left. At the corner rise left to the brow, and drop to a stile onto a T-junction. Turn left on traffic-free Hosticle Lane all the way down into Whittington, noting the very old Pearson House on the right. Go left, passing the church of St Michael the Archangel with its 15th century tower, and the Manor House of 1658. At a junction with the B6254, along to the right is the sadly derelict Dragons Head pub.

   Bear left out of the village, and after the last house take a gate on the right to head along a short hedgeside to a gate onto a concrete track-end. Don't follow it but advance to a gate/stile just ahead, and maintain this line down the hedgeside through two further gates to meet a firm track. Turn left on it, over a gentle brow and down to a fork. Bear left over a streamlet, along a hedgerowed way into a field. Continue with the hedge the short way to the wide-flowing Lune. Turn left over a stile to head upstream, remaining by the river all the way back. At the field-end the path drops to a stile onto the very bank: it runs delightfully on, through neighbouring stiles at the end before a final one above a concrete aqueduct. Though the right of way traces the fence to drop down at the end, common usage follows a riverbank path, merging at a gate. The last stage follows the river to a stile in a wall prior to a kissing-gate at Devil's Bridge's garish replacement. Re-cross the road to drop back into the amenity area.

*Whittington church*

# 19 LECK BECK

**4¾ miles from Cowan Bridge**

**Lovely beck scenery penetrates unfrequented fell country off the beaten track**

*Start* Village centre (SD 635764; LA6 2HS), village hall car park up side road behind shop
*Map* OS Explorer OL2, Yorkshire Dales South/West
*Access* Open Access (tiny section)

Cowan Bridge is a tiny village astride a busy main road, with a shop/tearoom and a Methodist chapel. By the sidelined old bridge is a former Clergymen's Daughters School attended by four of the Bronte sisters. From the main road bridge over Leck Beck, a stile on the village side sends a surfaced path upstream by gardens to pass under an arch of a viaduct on the former Clapham-Tebay railway. The path resumes pleasantly with the tree-lined beck to reach a small gate: keep right with the fence as a slim pasture opens out. When it narrows, a gateway on the right sends a wallside track the short way along to a corner stile onto a narrow lane in scattered Leck. Turn left, and ignoring two right branches, it ends at the handful of buildings at what was Leck Mill.

Forking into driveways take the left one, past the house and on to a gate/stile into a field. A cart track heads away through this into a longer field. After bridging a sidestream, fork left to a gate into attractive Springs Wood. Emerging at another gate, the grassy track runs delightfully on through an extremely long pasture, passing a wooden cabin midway before reaching a gate/stile at the end into Open Access land. The track rapidly drops to Leck Beck amid colourful country and increasing bracken. Though your onward route vacates the beck at a fork at the first streamlet, for now remain with it to witness its finest moment a little further. Quickly ending at a footbridge, cross to a thinner path heading briefly away before it turns sharp right for a couple of minutes through bracken to arrive at a gorge where a modest waterfall drops into the deep pool of Job's Dub. Beneath it the beck tumbles through stony slabs, a truly charming spot.

Back at the fork, take the upper path slanting briefly up to another fork. Take the thinner but very clear upper path rising near the streamlet to a fence-stile, and up through scattered trees to another onto a cart track. Turn right, rising away from the wood on your right to traverse grassy moorland slopes. Ending abruptly on the high point, a contrastingly faint grass way continues amid partly moist surrounds. Advance on to merge with the wall to reach a ladder-stile at the very end. Through the next stile you enter lush fields, and a gentle descent of Castle Hill enjoys big views ahead to the Bowland moors. From another stile continue down to a gate, and with Leck Mill appearing ahead, down to cross a stream. Just past it, a stile in the wall puts you back onto the outward route just short of Leck Mill. If not retracing steps, then at the first fork in the road, rise left to a crossroads and follow the access road ahead to Leck's tiny school. Keep to the right-hand perimeter of its grounds, around to a small gate into the car park of St Peter's church. Joining a road, turn right to a junction then left to return to the start under another railway arch.

*The upper reaches of Leck Beck*

# 20 FOURSTONES

**4¼ miles from High Bentham**

**Grassy moorland and gentle pastures play support to massive Three Peaks views and a local landmark**

*Start* Station Road, Bentham Bridge (SD 667687; LA2 7LH), roadside parking
*Map* OS Explorer OL41, Forest of Bowland & Ribblesdale

The little market town of High Bentham is a western outpost of Yorkshire just a dozen miles from Morecambe Bay. Cross the bridge on the Wenning and turn right on a drive. Forking before a caravan park, bear left to houses at Moulterbeck. Pass between buildings to a gate, then left across the field bottom to a stile into a wood. A path ascends narrow confines, past a waterfall before reaching a stile just before leaving the trees. Bear right the short way up to the start of an enclosed grass track, rising outside the clough edge to arrive at the rear of buildings at Brookhouse. Through a gate at a ramshackle barn take another in front, and from one on the right, a grass track climbs a slender enclosure to a facing gate at the top. Look back to appraise the Dales peaks of Gragareth, Whernside and mighty Ingleborough. Continue to a stile in a tiny section of wall, then rising to ease and run to a stile left of a modern barn. Just past this take a gate into the farmyard at Bowker House, and out on the drive onto Mewith Lane.

Cross to a gate to the left, and climb two fields (stile midway) to Flannagill. From a stile into its garden, turn along the house front up to a corner stile in the garden wall. Entering the grassy moorland of Bents a clear trod rises gently left, then a little more left onto an access road with a wall behind. Go briefly right to a junction, then right the short way to a wall corner. Here go left into an initially reedy morass, escaping to ascend a grassy spur to a forking drive. Across, a path rises the short way to the Great Stone of Fourstones, the walk's high point at 787ft/240m. Carried here by glacier at the end of the

44

Ice Age, hewn steps offer a simple ascent, its panorama embracing a great sweep of Three Peaks country and massive Lakeland skyline.

A path doubles back left to information panels on the Slaidburn road, which follow down towards Lane Head: before the cattle-grid take a drive right. Ending at a second house, advance a few strides to drop to a footbridge in the enclave of Burbles Gill. Up the other side, take the path slanting left down the grassy moor, becoming moister at the bottom to join an access road by a cattle-grid at a house at Holly Tree. Follow this down to Mewith Lane and go right for two minutes to turn down Sunny Bank's drive. Pass right of the farmhouse and along to a gate into a field. Through a gateway on the left, slant down the field to a gate, then down the hedgeside to a wall-stile. Drop towards the wooded bank below, and bear left to a bench overlooking Bowtham Wood falling to the Wenning.

Resuming to a stile/gate just below, the path slants across the field to Staggarths, with a novel stile into the yard. At the end, don't follow the drive out past the house, but go right into a field and cross diagonally to a kissing-gate near the river. Advance on the riverside, around a sharp bend to a gate in a wall, where go left along its near side to a gate/stile at the end. Now cross a tapering field to rejoin the river at the end. Through a wall-stile, cross to a stile/gate at an outer wall/hedge corner, and an enclosed path runs to a stile onto a back road. Turn right with the river to finish.   *Great Stone of Fourstones*

# 21                       WENNING'S BANKS

**3½ miles from Low Bentham**

**A gentle stroll linking two villages by the banks of an unsung river**

**Start** *Village centre (SD 649694; LA2 7DS), car park by old station*
**Map** *OS Explorer OL2, Yorkshire Dales South/West*
***or** OS Explorer OL41, Forest of Bowland & Ribblesdale*

    Low Bentham is a colourful village with the aptly named Sun Dial Inn and a Public Hall of 1804. Just out of the centre a riverside area comprises church, pub and school, passed near the end. Facing the Sun Dial at the junction, go left a few strides then turn left along an access road to pass beneath a railway arch. Turning sharp left, an enclosed path runs past a fishery to reach the River Wenning. A super path heads upstream, with an early glimpse of Ingleborough before reaching a lovely corner with a waterfall. Resuming, the path rounds a bend to a kissing-gate onto a cart track. This runs briefly beneath the railway before you take a kissing-gate to resume upstream. Passing a sewage works to enter a caravan park, advance on the site road to a junction with a bridge to your right. Go briefly left to a junction, then right to a gate out of the site. Follow Wenning Avenue away to ultimately reach Station Road at High Bentham, with the church on a knoll ahead.

    Turn right over the bridge and right on a driveway by the river. Quickly reaching a cattle-grid, take a concession path right on the riverside, crossing a footbridge at the end into an open area. Cross to a kissing-gate ahead, behind which a stile puts you into the caravan park you met earlier. Advance along the road ahead to a hedge-gap, with the bridge right and reception left. Advance straight on, bearing slightly left to a wall-gap, then left again to the main site road at a shower block. Pass to its right, and just a little further, a path goes left to a kissing-gate out of the site.

An enclosed path runs right, soon rising to a kissing-gate into a field. Go right, over a wall-stile and along the field edge. Dropping to a viewpoint for the waterfall, pass through a wall-stile and cross a streamlet to commence a lovely open section along the riverbank. Over an intervening wall-stile you reach a stile into trees, and a path passes two weirs to a river bend: here the path rises left onto a back road. With a driveway opposite, take a pair of gates left and follow a faint path along the fieldside outside the grounds. Beyond, cross to an outer fence corner, keeping left of it to a stile at the end. Resume with a fence and drain on your left to a stile, just beyond which is a stile/gate onto a road. Go right to a junction at the Punch Bowl Inn, and left over Church Bridge.

Just ahead on the left is the church of St John the Baptist with its old tower, alongside the old grammar school. From a stile on the right over the bridge, a path runs upstream the short way to pass beneath a rail viaduct. Ascend steps to a stile into a field and go briefly right onto a knoll, then bear left down across a reedy dip to a plank bridge. Rising right to a gate, follow a hedge right, down to a corner gate into houses. While the drive runs out to Greenfoot Lane, properly you take a gate on the right part way on, down a paddock to a gate into a house grounds and out via another onto a green. A cross of 1902 commemorates Edward VII's coronation. Turn right to a junction, then right back to the centre.

*The River Wenning above Low Bentham*

# 22 TATHAM & WENNINGTON

**4¾ miles from Melling**

**Two attractive villages linked by fieldpaths with good open views**

*Start* Village centre
(SD 598712; LA6 2RA),
roadside parking at Lodge Lane
*Map* OS Explorer OL2,
Yorkshire Dales South/West

Melling is an old village based around St Wilfrid's church with its 15th century tower. An old milestone and old guidepost are neighbours on the main street, while Melling Hall stands at the junction. Head south past the church (its yard avoids the road), and just after the Institute bear left up an access road to Melling Green. Don't advance to the house at the end, but bear left up a grass track to the top corner. Don't follow it over the sidestream but take a gate above: Ingleborough appears over to the left, with the Howgill Fells up the Lune Valley. Ascend the fieldside to the next gate, which defends a moist corner. Above this slant slightly right, a scant line of trees leading to a gate at the top. The Dales panorama has been joined by the more distant Lakeland Fells.

Bear right to join a hedge, and follow it up to a brow revealing Lodge Farm. Pass through the gate on your right, down to a stile and up to the farm. Pass right of all buildings and down the field to a stile at the bottom. Continue over a gentle brow with views to Bowland. Drop to a stile by a gate below, then on again down a large pasture with Rectory Wood to your left. To the right of a tree-lined streamlet at the bottom is a small gate onto an access road at a house. Descend this to the old church of St James the Less, and resume on the road out to cross Tatham Bridge on the River Wenning onto the B6480. The Tatham Bridge Inn is along to the left.

The main route goes left just a few yards then right down narrow Park Lane. Beyond a dip it climbs between hedgerows, through a gate at the top to level out in open pasture. Just a little further, take a stile on the left and cross to a gate midway along Coat Bank Coppice. A path runs through the slender wood to a stile back out. Drop down the sloping field to a corner gate, then through a stile/gate on your left. Head away to a gate into the yard at Overends, and bear right to pass the house front and out on the driveway. Quickly reaching a bend, from a gate in front slant right down the field (good prospect of Wennington Hall ahead) to a gate/stile onto a road. A short descent leads over the railway back onto the B6480. Go right past the station, over Wennington Bridge into the centre. This peaceful little village is based around a central green alongside the Wenning. Abutting the bridge is an old pound.

Turn left on Lodge Lane, out past Wennington Hall. Largely rebuilt in 1856 the building has a long history: boasting an impressive tower, it is currently a school. Immediately after, a small gate on the right sends a path through trees to a stile. A stiff pull up the field gains a domed crest, looking over the hall to Bowland and across to the Dales fells. From an old stone stile just ahead, head slightly left down the field to one between gates at the bottom, and head away along a fenceside to a stile onto a hedgerowed track. Turn left to emerge onto unkempt Melling Moor, becoming surfaced and meeting Lodge Lane again to re-enter Melling.

*Melling church*

# 23 GRESSINGHAM & THE LUNE

**4¾ miles from Arkholme**

**Two villages are linked by fieldpaths and a splendid section of river**

*Start* Village centre (SD 584719; LA6 1AU), roadside parking, village hall car park
*Map* OS Explorer OL7, English Lakes South East & OS Explorer OL41, Forest of Bowland & Ribblesdale

Arkholme is a pleasant street village of old houses running down to the River Lune. At its top end on the B6254 are the school, village hall and recently closed Bay Horse pub. Leave midway along Main Street by a short access track between substantial Poole House of 1674 and a house of 1693. Ignoring a gate at the end, go right on a short, enclosed path, and up a few steps into an outer garden. Cross to a stile ahead into a field, and a thin trod heads away. Towards the end bear left down to a stile alongside Bains Beck onto the B6254. Go briefly right past Bainsbeck House, then take a stile to pass outside the grounds to a stile/gate, and on to a gate at the end. Now bear gently left across a large field to a gate/stile after a streamlet left of a belt of trees. Head away with fence and stream on the left to a footbridge and stile at the end. Bear left up the field centre to a gate/stile, then on with a hedge to a small gate in front of Locker Hall. Cross a tiny enclosure to a gate ahead into the yard, and out onto Locker Lane.

With big views from the Howgill Fells to Ingleborough, turn left on the quiet road to meet the B6254. Go briefly right, and just past the entrance to Storrs Hall with its impressive tower, take a narrow gateway in the wall. A path runs through a belt of trees to a stile into a pasture. Bear right past a few trees to an outer fence corner, and on to a stile in the recess to its right. Bear right again up the field to a stile just beneath a protruding wood, then on to a corner stile/gate onto a road. Turn left for a steady descent into tiny

Gressingham, curving left onto the main street in front of St John the Evangelist's church with its Norman doorway. Keep left of the church, passing late 17th century Gressingham Hall and quickly out of the village as the road drops towards Loyn Bridge. Hornby Castle is seen down the valley. At a sharp right bend at the bottom, the road can be short-cut at a footpath sign on the left: if there's still no stile, then either remain on the road or climb the fence to cross the field to the near side of the fine triple-arched bridge.

An intermittent path traces the Lune upstream and will lead unfailingly to Arkholme, with little description needed. A stile out into a field after a first wooded section sends the way on beneath a sloping pasture back into trees, before long tracing a sidestream to a footbridge over it. From a stile behind, forge on through scrub to regain the river. Further, a pair of streamlets are crossed with Arkholme in view ahead. After a stile/gate, the river bends off as you advance with a fence on your right to a corner stile/gate. On the fence's other side you pass a cottage to a gate at the end, and a cart track rises onto a road-end at Arkholme. The first access road on the right rises to Chapel House to see the little church of St John the Baptist to your right: in the churchyard is the grassy knoll of Chapel Hill, site of 11th century Arkholme Castle. Return along the lane onto Main Street to finish.

*The River Lune below Arkholme*

# 24                    THREE RIVERS

**4 miles from Hornby**

**Two absorbing yet very contrasting villages with spells by a trio of rivers**

*Start* Village centre (SD 584685; LA2 6JT), car park by bridge
*Map* OS Explorer OL41, Forest of Bowland & Ribblesdale

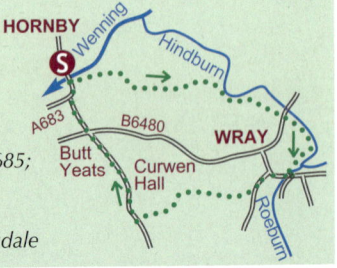

    Hornby is an elegant village split by the Wenning's final mile before entering the Lune. Around St Margaret's church with its octagonal tower of 1514 are the Royal Oak, Castle Inn, Post office/tearoom, shop and butchers. The originally Norman Hornby Castle was rebuilt in the mid-19th century, though a 16th century tower survives. From the bridge, head a few yards south and take a short lane left on the near side of the Institute. Through a yard, follow the concrete road to the river. As it bends off, the track runs an enclosed course with a view back to the castle above a wooded bank. At the end pass through a gate and take one on the right to cross a streamlet. With Ingleborough majestically appearing, bear left across the field to a fence-stile, and maintain this course through two further hedge-stiles to a corner gate by a wall. Over it is a section of the Wennington-Lancaster railway that closed in 1966.

    Go left on a grassy wallside track, and at the end cross the old line on your right by kissing-gates. Head off on a hedgerowed green path, at the end of which is a kissing-gate, with the River Hindburn ahead. Go right on the field edge to pick up a track at a gate, and on again, briefly, until a stile on the left keeps you by the river. From the next stile cross to sewage works, where an enclosed path outside its perimeter puts you onto its access track. Go left past the entrance, and bear right on a hedgerowed track running to a bridge at Meal Bank on the B6480 on the edge of Wray. Cross the road, not the bridge, and a good path resumes upstream. This quickly puts you into a field for a riverside stroll through sheep pasture. Bending around through a gate/stile, a kissing-gate just ahead puts a tightly-enclosed path onto the very bank at the confluence of the Hindburn and the Roeburn. Just a little further you trace the latter onto a green at Wray Bridge, across which is Bridge House Farm (café and gifts). Turn right along the street past attractive cottages and a Post office/shop to a junction just before Holy Trinity church. Along the street is the George & Dragon pub.

Go left up School Lane, steeply past the school to a bend. Look back over the village roofs to Three Peaks country, and up the Lune Valley to the Howgill Fells. From a gate on the right, follow a sunken way above the wall to a stile at a bend. Head away above Neddy Park Wood, passing through a kissing-gate to bear slightly left to a gate/stile. Rise gently away with a fence on your left to a brow, where a stile sends a part-enclosed way to a bridle-gate in front of a set of gates. From the central one keep straight on with a fence on your right all the way to a kissing-gate onto Moor Lane. Turn right, over a slight brow with Hornby Castle ahead, and down to an old cross at Curwen Hall Farm drive. Further, you drop to the B6480 at Butt Yeats, alongside a large cross base. Cross over along Station Road, over the old rail bridge and back into Hornby by way of a fountain of 1858.

*Hornby Castle from the River Wenning*

# 25 CROOK O'LUNE

**4½ miles from Caton**

**Level strolling on the bank of the wide-flowing Lune and an old railway**

*Start* Bull Beck (SD 542649; LA2 9NB), car park on A683 a long half-mile east of village
*Map* OS Explorer OL41, Forest of Bowland & Ribblesdale

From this popular car park with refreshments and WC, cross the road to the former railway line. Opened in 1850 to connect the West Riding towns with Morecambe, this section between Wennington and Lancaster closed to passengers in 1966. Turn left on its firm surface, and follow it for almost 1½ miles, en route bridging Artle Beck to reach Caton's picturesque Station House. A half-minute detour left on Station Road puts you in the village centre with the Ship Inn and Station pubs, and a shop. The railway continues on to a large bridge over the River Lune, with a view upstream to Ingleborough. Immediately across are steps up to Crook o'Lune car park, with WC and refreshments. At this popular spot the river performs a sharp dog-leg: a stone-arched bridge crosses one section, while twin old rail viaducts straddle both.

Remain on the railway path beneath the road bridge to the second river crossing. Immediately over, take a path dropping right to the bank, and pass under the bridge on a path upstream through trees. An early impasse forces you up wooden steps to emerge alongside the main road: the path resumes on the wood top before dropping back down steps to the river. It now shadows the Lune around the sharp curve of the Crook itself, emerging from trees at a footbridge on a streamlet and heading across an open pasture incorporating the Millennium Wood. After a branch to a bench the path quickly forks: keep left across the pasture near the river to a kissing-gate onto a road just short of the bridge.

From a bridle-gate opposite, don't follow the hard path to the railway, but drop left to a riverbank footbridge on a sidestream between the two massive bridges. Go right beneath the eastern viaduct to emerge into an open pasture, commencing a delectable walk upstream on a barely evident path. The wide-flowing river leads the eye to Ingleborough, with Caton Moor windfarm and Clougha Pike to the right. Passing a weir before crossing a neat footbridge on Artle Beck, the bank leads to the Waterworks Bridge. This massive aqueduct was built by Manchester Corporation to carry water from Thirlmere to their thirsty city. Beyond it is a seat with lovely views across the Lune to Aughton Woods.

Resuming, a delectable greensward leads to a sharp loop of the river. Not obvious until you reach it, it then becomes very obvious there's no option but to double back right down-valley, yet still upstream. Through a stile then around to a kissing-gate, the way curves round to another bend. At the next gate a cart track forms to lead past sheep pens. Just beyond, the main track leaves the river enclosed by hedgerows: don't follow it, but take the left branch through a gate to remain near the Lune. It quickly drops to its bank and expires, but simply continue upstream along the field edge. With the A683 ahead as the river swings left, go straight ahead the short way to a kissing-gate onto the old railway. Just two minutes or so to the right you reach the point where you joined it, so re-cross the road to finish.

*The River Lune at Crook o'Lune*

# 26 LITTLEDALE

**3¾ miles from Crossgill**

**Wooded surrounds in a hidden corner rich in springtime flora**

**Start** New House Farm (SD 553625; LA2 9EX), roadside parking on Littledale road to east, reached from Caton
**Map** OS Explorer OL41, Forest of Bowland & Ribblesdale

From the junction at the farm turn east on the road to Littledale, with big views across to Littledale Fell. Dropping through the hamlet of Crossgill, the farmhouse bears a 1661 datestone. Just past the drive to Littledale Hall is the former St Ann's church of 1751. At a hairpin bend beyond it, turn off right through a stile/gate onto a cart track between plantations. From a stile/gate at the end of the trees, a gentler track continues to a gate to approach a church in the middle of a field. Now merely a shell, this Free Church of 1849 was attached to nearby Littledale Hall. A solitary grave at the rear is the resting place of father and son Dodsons of the hall. Through a gate just beyond, the track forks: the main one drops to Littledale Hall, to which you shall return.

For now take the grassy left branch, winding up around the field top beneath trees. When the track goes through a gate, remain on the field top to a little gate into the top of a wooded bank: a delectable path now ambles above a May-time bluebell carpet. Emerging at a stile, a grand scene features Ragill Beck splashing along beneath woodland: your return route is below. For now contour on, crossing a streamlet and up the bank behind. From the fence corner above, rise just 30 yards to a super grassy path contouring across the bank, largely above bracken. When a variant bears left, your narrower continuation crosses a few reeds, remaining level before dropping at the end to a cart track in front of a footbridge on a sidestream. Ignore the bridge and turn right on the track, quickly joined by Ragill Beck for a pleasant stroll to a gate back into the wood. The bluebell display excels as your track runs on to leave by a stile/gate at the end. The grassy track advances on to cross a stone-arched bridge at Littledale Hall.

Rise left up the hard track, bearing right up through the farmyard. After the last barn, a gate on the right sends a grassy path upstream into the wooded confines of Foxdale Beck. Soon crossing by a footbridge, the path doubles back above the stream, quickly taking an easily missed left turn up wooden steps. The upper, ill-drained section leads to a stile into a field. Bear right along the gently rising hedgeside, crossing at a stile shortly after a wall takes over. Cross to Field Head Farm, passing right of the buildings onto the drive. Follow this away over a brow with magnificent Lakeland views: much closer is Caton Moor windfarm. After an early cattle-grid, turn right down the fenceside to a stile at the bottom corner. Head straight down the field to join an old wall leading to the barn at what was Bradley's Farm. An old green way leads down to a stile/gate into woodland. Joining a rough track, go left along the wood top to a stile/gate at the end, then a short way further back onto the farm road. Just yards to your right it joins a road at Udale Bridge. Don't cross but turn right over Fostal Bridge, passing a scout camp before a short pull up and along to New House.

*Springtime in Littledale*

# 27 CLOUGHA PIKE

**4 miles from Quernmore**

**An exhilarating climb through rugged terrain to a charismatic Bowland landmark: big views**

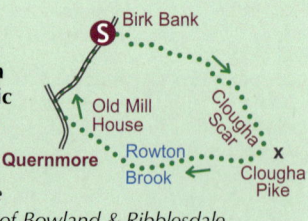

**Start** Birk Bank (SD 526604; LA2 9EP), car park on Rigg Lane
**Map** OS Explorer OL41, Forest of Bowland & Ribblesdale
**Access** Open Access land, no dogs

From a gate at the rear of the car park, a green track heads away towards rocky Birk Bank, the scene of long-abandoned quarrying. At an early fork bear right then right again, running to a gate. Don't use it but take the path left, using boards to cross a marsh. The path then runs with a stream, soon rising gently through gorse and oak. Leaving the trees, it climbs through bilberry bushes to a wall junction beneath a rocky knoll. From the right-hand stile a wallside path rises away, with Windy Clough to your left. At a near immediate fork take the right branch, rising through boulders to slant up the moor. Clougha's upper contours are soon fully revealed above Clougha Scar, as the path rejoins the wall to cross at a small gate. Rising only very gently to pass boulders and then a bouldery edge, the path crosses to further boulders beneath another wall. The broad path now rises ever gently right with the wall, through scattered boulders in glorious moorland surrounds.

The wall falters at the onset of a rocky edge, and a fence branches off left. Through a kissing-gate and adjacent fence-stile (or wall-gap just further), the broadening path quickly curves away from the fence, acquiring a natural, tilted stone floor to rise to a prominent cairn: the summit waits just beyond. An OS column at 1355ft/413m shares a platform with sprawling shelters built from the rash of stones. A level, heathery hinterland heads away from your 'pikeless' pike to Ward's Stone's great top beyond Grit Fell. Set back further left, Yorkshire's magnificent Three Peaks country must play second fiddle to the breathtaking spread of Morecambe Bay beyond the Vale of Quernmore, backed by the Lakeland Fells.

Leave by a clear, thinner path contouring away beyond the main shelter, within 40 yards bearing right down an inviting grassy groove. At its foot it drops right to gently descend the grassy moor, with an old wall over to the right. With minor reedy patches either side of a streamlet, it drops to a gate in a wall. While the right of way crosses Rowton Brook to resume down the other side, common practise uses the gate to take a grassy way down rough pasture to two gates in the next wall. From the right-hand one, re-enter open country to descend between wall and stream to a corner stile. A grass track descends the field parallel with the brook, crossing it at the bottom into Rooten Brook Farm. Pass between house and barns and down the drive, becoming enclosed at the bottom. On crossing the brook take an enclosed cart track right, and beneath a house it descends between walls outside the stream's wooded confines. Emerging into a field at the bottom, drop to a gate at Old Mill House, and follow its drive out past another house down onto Rigg Lane. Turn right for two minutes to a junction where Postern Gate Road continues ahead: here bear right on the continuation of Rigg Lane for a dead-straight return to the start.

*Clougha Pike*

# 28 ALDCLIFFE MARSH

**4¾ miles from Lancaster**

**An absorbing stroll from the historic castle to the tidal Lune**

**Start** The Castle (SD 474617; LA1 1YN), car parks
**Map** OS Explorer 296, Lancaster, Morecambe & Fleetwood

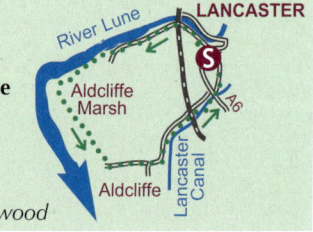

Lancashire's county town is an absorbing small city centred around Castle Hill, on which stand its iconic castle and priory church. The castle is known for its centuries-old prison, in service until as recently as 2011: its best known occupants were the hapless Pendle Witches, who were tried and hanged here in 1612. Open to visitors, there is a cafe in the courtyard. Facing the imposing 15th century gatehouse, go briefly right on the road to some steps rising to the priory church. At its far side turn right on a surfaced path to a small gateway, from where the path becomes enclosed to drop down past a grassy public space. Part way down, a path detours 100 yards right to inspect the Roman bath-house. At the bottom cross a tarmac way, down setts and then steps onto the road at St George's Quay.

Cross to the footway and go left alongside the wide-flowing River Lune. This remains your uncomplicated course for some time, passing converted warehouses, two pubs and the Maritime Museum based in the Custom House of 1764. Passing beneath the railway bridge of Carlisle Bridge, you divert from the road and remain on the cycle path with the river past assorted housing. Further, your path shadows the road with modern housing opposite. A tract of waste ground diverts you from the river for a spell, then as the houses end at the start of an industrial estate, a good path bears right into undergrowth. This now runs a lengthy course by the intermittently visible river, and a spell in denser greenery precedes emergence into the open, a lovely moment.

The path runs nicely on with the Golden Ball pub at Snatchems seen across the wide channel. Before long you rise left to a gateway on an embankment at the start of the big sweep of Aldcliffe Marsh. Look back over Freeman's Pools to see the church, castle, Ashton memorial, also Clougha Pike on the Bowland moors. The river is now barely visible as you bear right through a kissing-gate at the start of a super embankment path on Dawson's Bank. With the marsh outspread on your right, it runs for a full mile, the second half with the bird-friendly delights of Wildfowlers' Pools on your left. Ultimately you arrive at a kissing-gate where the path ends, putting you onto the end of Aldcliffe Hall Lane.

Cross the Lune Millennium cycle track on the course of the Lancaster-Glasson Dock railway, and head away on the tall-hedged lane. Entering exclusive Aldcliffe it rises to a T-junction: turn left for a few minutes to reach the Lancaster Canal. Go left on the towpath for a surfaced stroll into suburbia, passing beneath a rail bridge into the town proper. At the next bridge, Basin Bridge, pass under and turn up to cross it to a wider path for the final stretch on the other bank. Just past the well-placed Water Witch pub, take the path slanting right up to the main road. Go left, passing Penny's Hospital almshouses of 1720 and the adjacent Assembly Rooms of 1759. Reaching Market Street, go briefly left then right up Castle Hill to the castle.

*Pools at Aldcliffe Marsh*

# 29 SUNDERLAND POINT

**4½ miles from Middleton**

**An intriguing old hamlet at the very mouth of the River Lune**

***Start*** *Potts' Corner (SD 413571; LA3 3LL), beach parking at end of Carr Lane, 1½ miles south-west of village*
***Map*** *OS Explorer 296, Lancaster, Morecambe & Fleetwood*
***Access*** *Beware of high tide times*

At the start you gaze over extensive saltmarshes that support vast numbers of wading birds. Adjacent Shorefields Caravan Park has a beach shop. Facing the sea, turn left on a track close by the boundary fence. Immediately forking, keep right across the marsh, with the fence further off to the left now. Ahead are the Bowland moors. The fence is rejoined as the track ascends a concrete ramp to a gate. Ignoring this, remain on an intermittent marsh-side track beneath the fence. Further you pass Sunderland Brows Farm over the hedge to reach a gate beneath a bird-hide. Here is the start of The Lane, an excellent optional hedgerowed short-cut path into Sunderland. Behind the gate another gate accesses the hide, the domed Horizon Line Chamber, and just beyond, the very moving Sambo's Grave. This young slave arrived at Sunderland from the West Indies with his master in 1736, but died shortly after.

For the full experience return to the marsh-gate and resume outside the fence, an intermittent track fading before you reach a fence-gate. A couple of minutes further you pass beneath anti-erosion boulders to gain the tip of Sunderland Point, with the River Lune in front. Double back left on the stony shore to the exposed setting of Old Hall: a little path runs outside the garden to join the access road, which leads pleasantly into Sunderland. Once a busy port for the arrival of sugar, rum and tobacco from the West Indies, one thing that hasn't changed is the fact that it is cut off by tides twice a day. Advancing past the houses the access road briefly resorts to the beach, though a concrete path runs above it. Past further houses is a WC, immediately past which the road heads off across the marsh amid old boats. Don't follow it but take an access road left beneath the final house. As it rises to an embankment, bear right with the marsh-edge hedge to a stile onto the embankment.

Drop down and head diagonally away past a drain-end to a simple drain bridge near the corner. Across, head away with a hedge/drain on your left to a sturdier bridge at a drain junction. Resume on the other side of the drain/hedge to a bridge onto an access road, crossing over and along another drain-side to a bridge into a sheep pasture. Resume with the winding drain, and at its end bear left with the fence to a stile just short of the corner. Head away with a hedge on your left, beneath an embankment to a stile/gate at the end. This sends you on a raised path the short way to a stile onto the embankment. Go briefly right then drop left to a stile, then briefly right to a cart track. Follow this left along the hedgeside, curving round beneath the farm at Trailhome, and becoming firmer. With the farm road parallel to your right, take a stile in the hedge to join it, and go briefly left to another stile in the hedge.

Over this you rejoin the earlier track, going right a few yards to Trumley Farm's access road. Go very briefly left, and bear right on the short drive to Marsh Lea. Pass right of the buildings to a stile at the end, and go briefly left on a rough track to a path crossroads. From the kissing-gate on your left head away over the brow of this large sheep pasture, the walk's high point at a mere 33ft/10m. Bear gently right to a stile just short of the end. Go left to a corner, and briefly right to a stile/gate in a small recess in front of buildings. Go the left on the fieldside to a kissing-gate into the yard, then right on the short driveway out onto Carr Lane. Turn left to finish.

***Sambo's Grave***

# 30          HEYSHAM HEAD

**4¾ miles from Morecambe**

**A straighforward promenade - literally - to an old village and intriguing headland**

**Start** Midland Hotel (SD 428643; LA4 4BU), car parks
**Map** OS Explorer 296, Lancaster, Morecambe & Fleetwood

Morecambe's fine setting looks across its bay to the Lakeland Fells. From the iconic Midland Hotel facing the Stone Jetty, head south along the broad Promenade, noting that from the outset you could opt for the beach, tides permitting. Leaving the lively area behind, simply stroll on past the final buildings, with Heysham Head's knoll backed by a power station. Beneath grassy slopes you reach a fork: keep straight on an embankment path the short way to its terminus at Heysham. Steps climb to a path junction by a cafe: your return will commence here. Advance past the cafe onto Bailey Lane, then right a few strides to a junction with Main Street.

Turn right onto the stony beach (at high tide go up Main Street to the church). Go left beneath low cliffs and over rocky slabs under the churchyard wall. Quickly reaching a sandy cove, steps rise onto grassy Heysham Head. Joining a good path, go right through scrub to curve round to the crest of a cliff. Free of scrub it runs onto a brow, continuing above cliffs to pass through a wall-gap. Now broader and stonier, you soon reach a junction, where double back left on a similar path. This rises slightly and back through the wall into more open surrounds, to run to dramatically-sited 8th century St Patrick's chapel, with stone graves hewn from the rock. To its right a cobbled path runs onto a little lane by St Peter's church. Rejoining Main Street, on your right is the Royal Hotel, with a heritage centre beyond. To return drop left back to the cafe, and from the path junction ascend a tarmac path right to the broad upper one from earlier. Turn down this to rejoin the outward route, and retrace steps either by promenade or beach.

64